THE SECRET LIFE OF THE
YETI

by Benjamin Harper

Published by Capstone Press, an imprint of Capstone
1710 Roe Crest Drive, North Mankato, Minnesota 56003
capstonepub.com

Library of Congress Cataloging-in-Publication Data is available on the Library of
Congress website.

ISBN: 9781669004233 (hardcover)
ISBN: 9781669040477 (paperback)
ISBN: 9781669004196 (ebook PDF)

Summary: Readers take a look into the secret life of the yeti to uncover surprising
facts, including the cryptid's mountain home, its fur color, and more.

Editorial Credits
Editor: Abby Huff; Designer: Heidi Thompson; Media Researcher: Jo Miller;
Production Specialist: Tori Abraham

Image Credits
Alamy: BFA, 29, Chronicle, 21, Classic Image, 11, Dale O'Dell, 27, Historic
Collection, 13, Jeff Morgan 16, 24 (portrait); Getty Images: Popperfoto, 19, Royal
Geographical Society, 20, VICTOR HABBICK VISIONS/SCIENCE PHOTO LIBRARY,
5; Shutterstock: Brian A Jackson, 12, Cactus Studio, Cover, 28 (Yeti), CloudyStock,
7, 9 (Yeti), Daniel Prudek, 23, e71lena, 17, Insdesign86, 28 (glasses, hat, mustache),
Kitnha, 8, luma_art, 22, mmckinneyphotography, 16, Nanisimova, 18, Oakview
Studios, 10, Photo Volcano, 9 (mountain), RikoBest, 15, Savvapanf Photo, 24 (hair),
V_ctoria, Cover (headphones), Vishnevskiy Vasily, 25, Wanida_Sri, 14

Design Elements
Shutterstock: Kues, kelttt

Printed and bound in China. PO5132

TABLE OF CONTENTS

Words in **bold** are in the glossary.

MEET THE YETI

Ready for a snow day? Chill with the coolest **cryptid** around. The yeti! These hairy **creatures** live in the frosty mountains of Asia. They've been stomping around for a long time. Find out all about the yeti's secret life!

FACT

Cryptids are animals some people believe are real. But science can't show for sure they exist.

SNOW BEAST BUDDIES?

Are you a yeti know-it-all? Can you guess the cryptid's:

1. Home?

2. Fur color?

3. Foot length?

4. Height?

5. Most famous nickname?

ANSWERS

1. The Himalayas, a mountain range in Asia

2. Brown

3. 13 to 32 inches

4. About 6 feet

5. The **Abominable** Snowman

MOUNTAIN MYSTERY

Yetis aren't afraid of heights. They live in the snowy Himalayas. This mountain range is in southern Asia. Here you can find Mount Everest. It's the highest mountain peak in the world! Would you go on a hike to visit the yeti?

Himalayas

OLD STORIES

People in the Himalayas have many yeti **legends**. Stories go back thousands of years. In 326 BCE, Alexander the Great led his armies into what's now India. He heard about the furry creature. He wanted to see it. No luck! **Locals** said the yeti couldn't live away from its high-up home.

WHAT DID YOU CALL ME?

In 1921, a journalist talked with a British group climbing the Himalayas. The group had seen strange footprints. Locals said the prints were made by *metoh-kangmi*. It roughly means "man-beast snowman." But in his article, the journalist called the beast Abominable Snowman. It's been a yeti nickname ever since!

FACT
The new name and footprint reports made the yeti more well-known in Western countries.

DAILY NEWS
EXTRA!
EXTRA!

the British climbers

LET'S BUILD A SNOWMAN

You know what a regular snowman looks like. But what about an abominable one? Many **witnesses** say yetis aren't white at all. Instead, they have brown hair. A yeti's long fur keeps it warm on hikes.

Abominable? I think you mean adorable.

A yeti walks on two legs like a human. But reports say it has a face like an ape. The cryptids stand about 6 feet tall. They have lots of muscle. Their bulky bodies likely weigh 200 to 400 pounds.

Um, why is that ape walking like that?

FROSTY FEET

Yetis don't need boots to play in the snow. They stomp with their bare feet. Many people have reported seeing footprints in the Himalayas. Some of the smallest prints are 13 inches long. One of the biggest comes in at 32 inches.

1951 yeti footprints

WILD FOR YETIS

In 1951, British climber Eric Shipton was hiking on Mount Everest. He spotted something odd in the snow. It was a trail of huge footprints! He snapped photos of the prints. The pics made headlines around the world. The yeti became a global hit.

Eric Shipton in the Himalayas

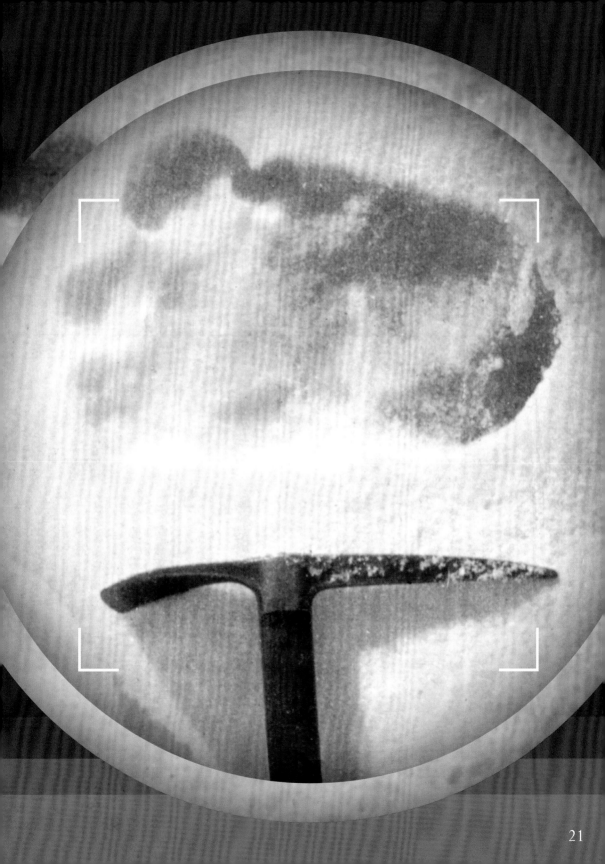

THE HUNT IS ON

Since the 1950s, at least four major searches have looked for yetis. None have turned up firm **proof** of a mountain beast. But in 1959, a U.S. monster hunter did get a stinky item. His group found what they believed was yeti poop! Pee-yoo!

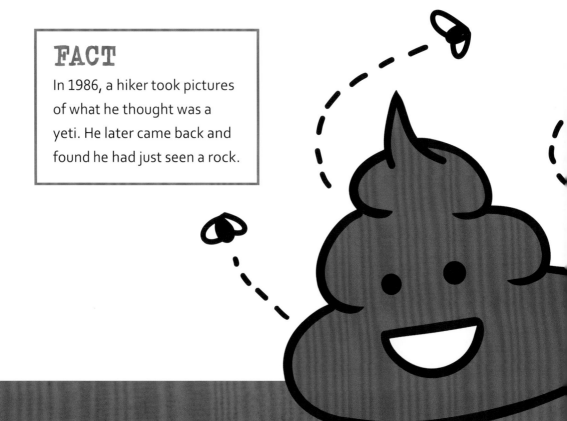

FACT

In 1986, a hiker took pictures of what he thought was a yeti. He later came back and found he had just seen a rock.

SERIOUS SCIENCE

Got proof? In 2013, British scientist Bryan Sykes put out a call for yeti hairs. People sent in cryptid fur. Sykes tested 37 samples. Turns out, all the hairs matched known animals. Many belonged to bears. Could the yeti be more bear than ape?

Bryan Sykes

> **FACT**
>
> In 2011, Scottish scientists tested what was said to be an old yeti finger. It was actually human.

AROUND THE WORLD

Do yetis have family around the globe? In North America, people have spotted Bigfoot. This cryptid has long, brown fur. It has BIG feet! Sound familiar? Some people think Bigfoot and yetis are the same kind of animal. Others say the yeti is shorter. Are the cryptids cousins? Maybe!

FACT
Every continent except Antarctica has had sightings of hairy apelike cryptids.

IT'S SNOW TIME!

Yetis live in Asia, but they pop up in Hollywood. The cryptid stars in the holiday special *Rudolph the Red-Nosed Reindeer.* It's in movies, such as *Abominable.* It's even in a Bugs Bunny cartoon!

If you follow snowy footprints, will you meet the yeti in person? What do you think?

Cute movie, but they got my hair all wrong!

GLOSSARY

abominable (uh-BOM-uh-nuh-buhl)—so bad or unpleasant that it causes hatred or makes you feel sick

creature (KREE-chur)—a strange animal

cryptid (KRYP-tid)—an animal that has not been proven to be real by science

legend (LEJ-uhnd)—a story passed down through the years that may or may not be entirely true

local (LOH-kuhl)—a person who lives in a certain place

proof (PROOF)—something that helps show a statement or idea is true

witness (WIT-ness)—a person who has seen or heard something

READ MORE

Beccia, Carlyn. *Monstrous: The Lore, Gore, and Science Behind Your Favorite Monsters.* Minneapolis: Carolrhoda Books, 2020.

Colson, Mary. *Bigfoot and Yeti: Myth or Reality?* North Mankato, MN: Capstone Press, 2019.

Vale, Jenna and Laura Anne Gilman. *Tracking the Yeti.* New York: Rosen Publishing, 2018.

INTERNET SITES

Kidadl: Amazing Abominable Snowman Name, What It Looks Like and Where It Is!
kidadl.com/fun-facts/amazing-abominable-snowman-name-what-it-looks-like-and-where-it-is

Mocomi: Yeti a Mysterious Creature
mocomi.com/yeti/

PBS: The Crazed Hunt for the Himalayan Yeti
pbs.org/video/the-crazed-hunt-for-the-himalayan-yeti-f396zr/

INDEX

ABOUT THE AUTHOR

Benjamin Harper lives in Los Angeles where he edits superhero books for a living. When he's not at work, he writes; watches monster movies; and hangs out with cats Marjorie and Jerry, a betta fish named Toby, and tanks full of rough-skinned and eastern newts.